SENT

Contemporary epistolary poems

by

Nigel Kent

First published 2025 by The Hedgehog Poetry Press,

5 Coppack House, Churchill Avenue, Clevedon. BS21 6QW

www.hedgehogpress.co.uk

Copyright © Nigel Kent 2025

The right of Nigel Kent to be identified as the author of this work has been asserted in accordance with the Copyright, Designs and Patents Act 1988. All rights reserved. No part of this publication may be reproduced, stored in or introduced into a retrieval system, or transmitted in any form, or by any means (electronic, mechanical, photocopying, recording or otherwise) without prior written permissions of the publisher. Any person who does any unauthorised act in relation to this publication may be liable for criminal prosecution and civil claims for damages.

ISBN: 978-1-916830-46-2

Contents

Letter of Resignation 7
Letter I'd Like to Send 8
Job for Life 10
Love Letter #1 12
Memories 14
Ritual 16
Picture Perfect? 17
Parting 18
July 3024 20
Election Algorithm 22
Open Letter from an Anonymous Refugee 24
Missing 25
Fairytale 26
What's in a Name? 27
Secrets 28
Normal Service 30
Away from Home 32
Postcard from Murano 34
Note to Self 35
Facebook Message to a Festival Headliner 36

Acknowledgements 38
Thanks 38

"I have now attained the true art of letter-writing, which we are always told, is to express on paper exactly what one would say to the same person by word of mouth."

Jane Austen

For Kerry, Holly, Annie, Archie and Lyra

LETTER OF RESIGNATION

Thank you for your concern
but there is no place
for the progeny of
Courtesy and Accuracy
in today's workplace.
I have decided not
to return to work
and, anyway, as you know,
our team has been downsized:
much-abused Colon, Semi-Colon, Comma
all judged surplus to requirements,
and Upper Case,
the model of decorum,
summarily dismissed for SHOUTING.
Then there's Words, of course -
the produce we prepared
and plated up
to nourish readers -
no longer harvested,
but left to rot.
Rare heritage words
neglected in favour of
common varieties
that may fill but do not feed.
I now idle away my days
sitting silently
in the Residents' Lounge
of the Home for the Written-Off,
consoling myself with memories
of when words were kept,
listening to stressed Vowels
howl for revenge on
the callous thmbs of txtrs
and watching withdrawn Nouns
silently mouth their resentment
at the relentless rise of the emoji.

LETTER I'D LIKE TO SEND

after Edward Hopper's 'Office at Night'

Dear Mr Rogers

I want you to know

that it is not my job to buy your wife flowers,
make you coffee just the way you like it
or light your damned cigarettes for you.

I want you to know

that it is many years since I was a 'baby'
and despite my porcelain complexion
I never have been and never will be a 'doll'.

I want you to know

that I do not need you to approve
the cut of my dress, or the colour of my lipstick,
or tell me that my legs look 'so much finer' with high heels.

I want you to know

that you're not fooling anyone
when you let papers slip to the floor
and insist I keep current files in the lowest drawers.

I want you to know

that I think you're two bits short of a buck,
a bum, a knucklehead, a louse,
a heel, a misogynistic loser   (*Look it up yourself!*).

I want you to know all this

but what's a woman to do
without a dime to her name
living alone in New York?

So I just lap it up and purr.

Kat.

JOB FOR LIFE

Promotional email

Are you interested
in a life-changing, unsalaried post?

We are offering you
a unique opportunity
to work twenty-four-hour shifts
every day of the year,
with no provision for breaks,
in a position that offers
unparalleled job security,
for once contracted
there are no circumstances
under which your employment
can be terminated.

We are seeking applicants
from all walks of life.
There are no specifications
regarding qualifications,
and previous experience
is not essential,
though we have found candidates
with a working knowledge
of peacekeeping, conflict-resolution
and animal husbandry
most suited to the post.

All we ask from you
is a commitment
to your professional development,
taking up the daily opportunities
for on-the-job learning.

In return, we will guarantee
you receive frequent
feedback and advice
from self-appointed experts
in this complex field,
namely politicians, B list celebrities,
neighbours and your in-laws.

So, if you're an angel,
a saint, a martyr,
or just a super-hero,
who never sleeps,
apply today!

For video guidance
on how to make your application
visit our website:
www.soyouwannabeamummyoradaddy.org.uk.

Over 18's only.

(Please note that it takes
approximately nine months
to process applications.)

LOVE LETTER #1

Yes, of course, there were others:

    a childhood sweetheart
    who turned dreams sour;
    a flirty uni girl
    who mistook me
    for Mr Darcy,
    a musician who wearied
    of my attempts
    to play the many variations
    of her tune.

but you were the one

    who saw clearly
    the reason for hesitance,
    for the absence of bouquets
    and boxes of chocolates;

    who stretched out your arms
    to catch me
    before I knew
    I was falling;

    who cleared away
    the clutter from the past
    so it couldn't trip us up;

    who sealed our future
    with certainty,
    leaving no questions unanswered;

and who taught me
about home and family,
making 'you' and 'I'
into 'we' and 'us'

so that the ordinary
became extraordinary,
the imperfect perfect,
the broken whole again

with just a word,
a look, a smile, a kiss.

Once upon a time.

MEMORIES

Handwriting a thank you card

What a day!
So many memories
                that no amount
                of Photoshopping can erase:

the venue
                the Château des Fous, where plastic princesses
                purchase packaged fairy tales;
the gown
                a sheath of sequins, silk and lace
                that signposted too much territory
                to the stumbling survivors of the stag;
the bridesmaids
                whose painted smiles could not
                conceal the envy tattooed
                on their fake-tanned faces;

the vows
                breathy words that leant unsteadily
                on lyrics from old songs
                and soured the air with vinegary hyperbole;

the first dance
                a riot on the dance floor
                of jerks and twerks that the unrelenting spray
                of wine-soaked jeers could not quell;

your wonderful parents
                so watery-eyed, as they watched the air-bound
                explosions
                of glittering gold vanish in puffs of smoke
                that stank of burned bank notes.

Thank you,
we won't forget
your special day

*when notably your guest of honour, Love,
failed to make an appearance.*

RITUAL

DM to her best friend

His last gift to me,
the same for twenty years:
an album of family photos.
'The latest annal
of our family history!' he declared,
passing it proudly
round the table
to our family and friends,
who handled it
like some precious relic,
or ancient manuscript,
hands wiped clean with serviettes
to handle pages by their edges,
studying every picture,
and asking questions,
as if each held
some timeless truth,
but when he handed
the album on to me
I left it closed;
I know that truth's not found
in practised smiles and poses
it lies in what's been filtered out.

PICTURE PERFECT?

A text message

u alwys sd
i ws the whte spce
that dfned u,
tht gve u shpe,
tht i ws yr lfes
lght & shde,
the 1 who gve u
the prprtion & prspctv
tht ud lacked

so y did u leve me
scrwed up in a bll
upon the flr?

PARTING

DM to ex

To span the void,
of another night without you
I chose a documentary:
the separation of conjoined twins,
just ten years old.

Born the same month
we were married.

One to be sacrificed
so the other could survive,

thrive

though the condemned sister
was no parasite;
they shared a heart.

The cut
that killed
to save,
-decisive, final -
could not excise the love
that flowed like blood
between them,
the bond
that made them one.

They wrapped the chosen
one in bandages,
said time would be her nurse,
but there was no cure
for the suffering
she must endure,
grief clinging to her chest,
its nails sunk deep
in stolen flesh.

The closing shot focussed
on the sadness
in her fractured face

and I could not help
       but think of
              me

         and

         you.

JULY 3024

Dear Former Tenant

Your application for accommodation
has been refused.

Whilst we are not obliged
to justify our position,
we would like to state
that your previous occupancy
has led to this decision
and makes it improbable
that it would change
if subject to appeal.

Your failure to take reasonable
and proper care of our property
prior to your eviction
is well-documented
and it has taken many centuries
to make good your vandalism
and clear the waste you dumped
on your neighbours' doorsteps.

We expect our tenants
not to do anything
that causes nuisance
or annoyance to others.
Yet your casual disregard
of this obligation
drove innumerable fellow residents
from their long-held homes
and devastated the lives of millions,
many of whom
we will never see again.

In addition, you failed to heed
our frequent warnings,
continuing to abuse
and misuse your accommodation.
Your tenancy agreement
explicitly stated that our property
is for residential purposes only,
prohibiting use for personal profit
and limiting the number of occupants
in the interests of health and safety.
Terms and conditions
you wilfully chose to ignore.

We, at Planet Earth, do appreciate
the desperation that must have driven
you across the Galaxy
to beg for a second chance
of a permanent home
but please understand,
Humankind,
when we say

sod off
and don't come back!

ELECTION ALGORITHM

Emailed instructions from Party Headquarters
to Parliamentary Candidates

Begin
        with a salesman's
smile.

Hold
        the camera's eye.

Frown
to convey   seriousness
      concern
           appreciation.

Wrap promises
           in layers
of sincerity.

Redact
      small print.

Remove
      price tags.

Trash other parties'
         offerings.

Repeat on a loop

till

votes secured,
victory achieved

when
memories can be wiped
replaced with
        government upgrades,

guaranteed
        to deliver
improved protection
        (*for the powerful*)
    productivity
        (*for big business*)
    prosperity
        (*for the rich*)

upgrades no longer
    compatible
with voters' hopes

now rendered
        obsolete,
ready for

        scrapping.

OPEN LETTER FROM AN ANONYMOUS REFUGEE

January 2023

You call us invaders
yet we come in peace.
Can't you see how
willingly we surrender
to your forces waiting
on the beach?

Yet you line us up
like criminals to form
a screen to hide
the queues at A&Es
and the hungry homes
that shiver
through the winter.

You pin contempt upon us,
force us to wear it
through the city's streets
to incite the ire
of your despairing
and dispossessed.

You cast us adrift
in a bureaucracy holed
by hypocrisy where
buoyant hopes
list and sink
under waves of delays.

We travelled long and hard
to find protection, not persecution,
employment, not exploitation,
a home, not hostility,
yet you trade us for votes
with your currency of lies.

MISSING

A handbill

Police are appealing
for information regarding
the whereabouts
of public servant, Truth.
Last seen ejected
from the House of Commons
for whistleblowing,
concerns were raised
when Truth failed
to appear at yesterday's Public Inquiry.
Truth is described as plain,
sometimes awkward,
yet easily recognisable.
Members of the public
are asked to keep an eye open,
but not to approach,
as Truth may prove
difficult to handle.
The public should report
any sightings immediately
for fears are rising
regarding the safety
of this respected national figure
following the recent
unexplained disappearance
of close associates,
Honour,
Honesty,
and Hope.

FAIRYTALE

*A note for the boy leaning against
the wall of the pit of the Globe Theatre
June 2023*

I knew you by the blazer
not yet threadbare enough
to keep your mum awake.
I'd suffered one like it once.

You were slumped
against the wall of the pit,
weary of ducking words
projected from the stage.

You wanted to flee the scene-
for you seek salvation in your feet,
not in your wits -
though you did not know which way to go.

You were as lost as Helena and Lysander
on whom you'd turned your back
but there's no Google Map
to guide bedsit boys like us.

We must rub the potion from our eyes
that tells us to know our place,
see words as chinks,
offering a glimpse of the other side
and use them as footholds
to climb from our estate.

WHAT'S IN A NAME?

A card to Lyra on her naming

The name we give you
is not a label
to hang around your neck
to tell you what you are
or what we want you to become.
You must define yourself
and like your other features
the meaning of your name
will grow and change in time.
And when we use that name
we will not think
in terms of a single word,
but of a language
that you will teach us how to speak,
which tells the story
of the moments we have shared,
of the feelings we have felt:
a language as individual
as the fingerprints
left upon the key
we used to open the door
to invite you into our lives.

SECRETS

DM to mother

The name was the same,
age looked right
and there was something
familiar about the face
that had vanished
by the time
I was five.

The man you call
'a waste of space' -
hazardous waste
you'd isolated,
wrapping truth
in years of silence,
and sealed in a box
labelled, 'Do Not Open.
Injurious to Health.'

Seeing him again
broke the seals,
let the contents leak.
A caustic liquid,
that corroded
everything it touched,
.
and though I tried
to neutralize the toxic spill
by days out with the kids,
and a double gin or two,
I could not dilute
the acid in the residue'

Only you
had the means
to clean up
this mess.

Yet today
when you finally confessed,
the truth burned
a hole
which will never
close.

NORMAL SERVICE

A Christmas letter to Archie, 2023

Thank you for your letter, Archie.

How pleasing to read
that your parents
have only had to tell you off
once this month!

That makes it even more difficult
to write this letter to inform you
that we are unable
to fulfil your Christmas wishes.

Due to the actions
of the animal rights lobby
all reindeer have been grounded
until further notice,
and Santa's legal commitment
to reduce his carbon footprint
means alternative motorised
modes of transport are not viable.

You may also be aware
from current news reports
that international present deliveries
have become fraught with difficulties:
visa requirements at national borders,
post-Brexit customs licences
and heavy export duties
have resulted in significant costs and delays,
making it impossible to deliver
presents in a single night.

To make such matters worse, parents,
like yours, have installed log burners,
replacing traditional chimneys
with narrower, hotter metal flues,
which the Health and Safety Executive
has ruled must not be used
to enter any domestic premises,
even in exceptional circumstances.

For the above reasons,
we regret to inform you
Santa is unable to make
his traditional Christmas Eve delivery
this year.

We thank you for your patience
until we are able to develop
an alternative service.

To that end Santa is currently
in negotiations with Amazon
for 2030.

Happy Christmas!

AWAY FROM HOME

A WhatsApp message

Today

I parked
the pull of home
on the bank
of the river

allowed
the consoling pings
of your texts
to sink
in the wash
of water

compelled
the comfort
of memories
to sidestep
past me.

I busied myself
tending words
I'd gathered
so that they'd ripen
into phrases
to feed
conversations,

before submitting
to the spring
sunshine,
allowing it
to soften
and melt
the week's
solitude

until the shadows
yawned and stretched
across the concrete
concourse towards

tomorrow.

POSTCARD FROM MURANO

There are no mad dogs
at midday in Murano
just two stray Englishmen,
having landed at the jetty,
wafting maps like fans
that offer scant relief
against the furnace heat,
hot enough to make stone melt
and slide like molten glass
into the cool lagoon
beneath their burning feet
like some Dahlian dream,
to ruin the locals' *riposo*
in homes that gasp for breath.
The air, stretched tight,
has tethered panting dogs to shade,
stolid hostages
of the tyranny of heat,
ears twitching as they listen
with their owners
for the snap to set them free
but hearing only
the angry rattling
of bolts on café doors
and English voices complaining
about closing times, conveniences,
and Venetian cups of tea.

* *riposo* the Italian equivalent of a siesta

NOTE TO SELF

We can't repair
a tear in silk
without the stitches
being seen.

Neither can we glue
a mirror split in two
and think it will
reflect the same.

Nor fix the crease
that spoils the corner
of the page
by smoothing it away.

Perhaps we should
embrace the breaks,
the wear and tear
the damage done.

Celebrate the cracks
and chips and nicks
with lacquer
and with gold.

Find a beauty
in brokenness
and not restore,
discard or start anew.

FACEBOOK MESSAGE TO A FESTIVAL HEADLINER

*"Most people ignore most poetry,
because most poetry ignores most people."
Adrian Mitchell.*

With the confidence
of an evangelist
you strode onto the stage
to share your latest verses
with rhythms that mesmerised
and images that startled,
fizzled, flashed and flared.
We lauded you with applause,
beguiled by your promise
to light the hidden path
through the tangled labyrinth
we let you lead us to,
where all sense was lost.
Yet when we strained
against the darkness,
it would not yield its secrets
to the shower of waning sparks
that fell at your retreating feet.

ACKNOWLEDGEMENTS

Versions of some of these poems have appeared in: *Fall*, Nigel Kent (Hedgehog Poetry Press, 2023); *Dreich 100*, Various Artists (Hybriddreich, 2024); *A Little Black Book of Summer Poems*, Various Artists (Hedgehog Poetry Press, 2024); *Writing a Poem On A Cornflake Up A Ladder in the Tate Modern*, Various Artists (Hedgehog Poetry Press, 2023); *Paris Reflected*, Nick Browne and Nigel Kent (Independently Published, 2023).

THANKS

To Kerry, Holly, Annie, Robin, Tina, Mike, Wendy, Nick, Caroline, Stephen, John, Judy, Simon and Malcolm, who are tireless in their support.

To the Open University Poets with whom many of these poems have been shared and commented upon.

To John for his careful proof-reading.

To Barbara, Polly, Susan and Karen for their endorsements.

To Mark whose selfless commitment to providing opportunities to poets like me is unparalleled.